B49 081 364 8

KU-200-681

WITHDRAWN FROM THE ROTHERHAM PUBLIC LIBRARY

Helping Hands

At the Hospital

Chris Fairclough
and Louise Morrish

WAYLAND

ROTHERHAM LIBRARY &
INFORMATION SERVICES

J610.737

B49 081 3648

OES   431 301

First published in 2008 by Wayland

Copyright © Wayland 2008

Wayland,
Hachette Children's Books
338 Euston Road
London NW1 3BH

Wayland Australia
Level 17/207 Kent Street
Sydney, NSW 2000

Managing Editor: Rasha Elsaeed
Editor: Katie Powell
Design: Ruth Cowan
Commissioned photography: Chris Fairclough

All rights reserved. Apart from any use permitted under UK
copyright law, this publication may only be reproduced,
stored or transmitted, in any form, or by any means with prior
permission in writing of the publishers or in the case of
reprographic production in accordance with the terms of
licences issued by the Copyright Licensing Agency.

British Library Cataloguing in Publication Data:

Fairclough, Chris
At the hospital. - (Helping hands)
  1. Hospitals - Medical staff - Juvenile literature
  I. Title
  610.7'37069

ISBN: 9780750252454

Printed and bound in China

Wayland is a division of Hachette Children's Books, an
Hachette Livre UK company.

Acknowledgements
The author and publisher would like to thank the staff at the
Basingstoke and North Hampshire NHS Foundation Trust for
their help and participation in this book.

The website addresses (URLs) included in this book were
valid at the time of going to press. However, because of the
nature of the Internet, it is possible that some addresses may
have changed, or sites may have changed or closed down
since publication. While the author and Publisher regret any
inconvenience this may cause the readers, no responsibility
for any such changes can be accepted by either the author
or the Publisher.

Contents

Words printed in **bold** are explained in the glossary.

The team

We work at a hospital. A hospital is where people go to get treated if they are ill or injured. Doctors, nurses and other **specialists** work at the hospital to help people get better.

▲ We are **doctors**.

▲ I am a health care assistant.

▲ We are **nurses**.

This is the main entrance to the Basingstoke and North Hampshire Hospital. ▶

▲ We are **hospital play specialists.**

▲ We are **ancillary staff**.

▲ We are **radiographers**.

Reception

When patients arrive at the hospital they must first go to reception. A nurse will **register** all new patients.

▼ I welcome Susannah and her mum to the hospital.

Susannah has come to hospital for an operation. We will follow her progress to see what goes on inside the hospital.

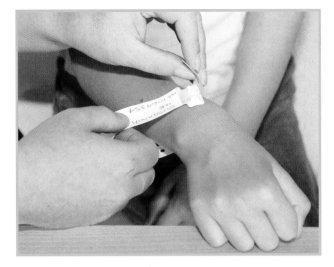

▲ Susannah has her identity nameband fitted. This shows her name and date of birth.

▼ I write Susannah's details on a form.

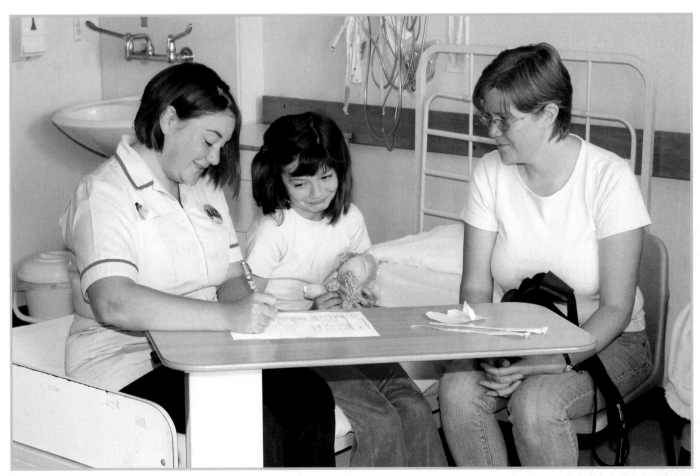

The children's ward

When children come to hospital, they stay in the children's ward. One of their parents can stay overnight as well if they would like to.

◀ I give Susannah her breakfast each morning.

Susannah's mum has a cup of tea in the Family Room kitchen. ▼

The children's ward has a special area for children to play in. Patients and their brothers and sisters can play here.

Susannah has found lots of toys in the play room. Other children play there, too ▼

Hospital play specialists

A hospital play specialist makes sure children are happy while they are in hospital. They are on hand to explain what is going to happen in the ward.

The hospital play specialists at this hospital play games with the children to make them feel at home.

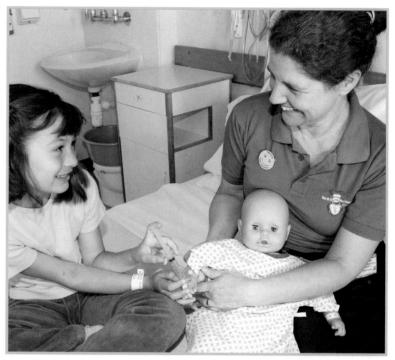

▲ I use a doll to show Susannah what to expect during her operation.

◄ Susannah and I have fun making a colourful picture for her mum.

What to take when staying in hospital:

* Comfortable clothes for night and day wear
* Dressing gown and slippers
* Items for washing, such as towel, flannel, sponge, soap
* Toothbrush and toothpaste
* Hairbrush
* A favourite toy and books
* Any school work
* Any medicines that you are taking

▼ I enjoy a pretend drink with Susannah in the play area.

Doctors

There are many doctors in the hospital. They visit patients every day to make sure they are getting better.

I am checking Susannah's breathing with a **stethoscope**. ▶

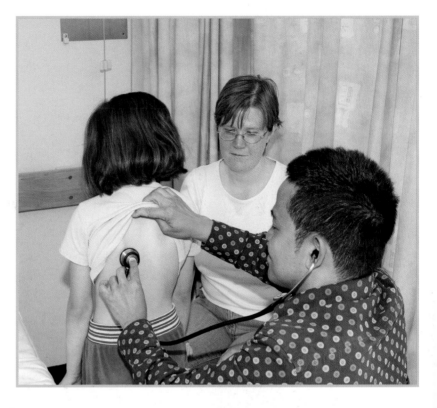

We are discussing a patients' progress after an operation. ▼

Doctors work **shifts** so that there is always a doctor on the ward in case there is a problem.

What to do in an emergency at home:

* Do not move the person who is hurt.
* Dial 999 on a telephone.
* Ask for an ambulance.
* Give them your address.
* Say what has happened.
* Wait for the ambulance to arrive.

As a doctor, I need to check **x-ray** images for each patient. ▼

Nurses

Nurses work with doctors to make sure patients get the care and treatment they need.

We keep in touch with patients' relatives by telephone. ▶

I apply an **anaesthetic** cream to Susannah's hand to make it **numb**. A doctor can then insert a tube called a **cannula** into Susannah's **vein** and she shouldn't feel it. ▼

The nurses in the children's ward are trained to look after children of all ages. They do many jobs to make sure children are comfortable.

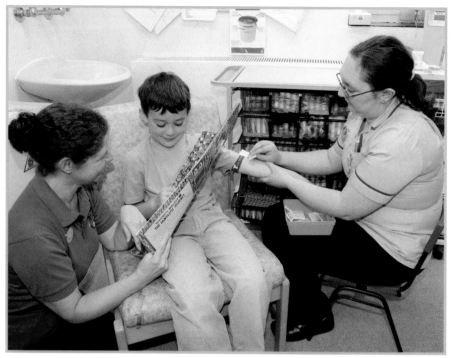

▲ I am taking a **sample** of Mark's blood for testing. A hospital play specialist distracts him with a book.

▼ We change the bed covers every day to keep the hospital clean.

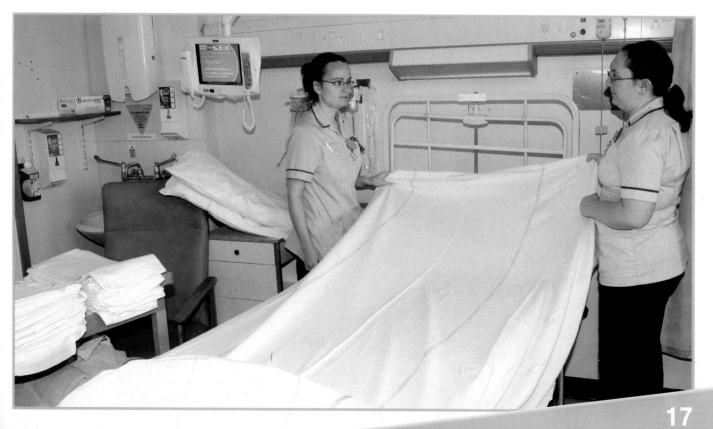

Ancillary staff

Many other people work
in the hospital and the
children's ward.

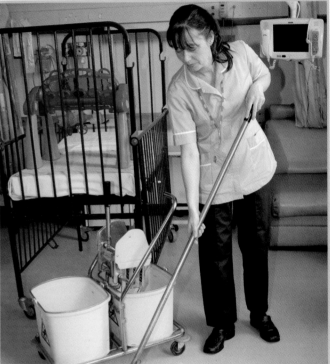

I am a housekeeper. It is
my job to keep the ward
clean and tidy. ▶

As a health care assistant, I help to
prepare food for patients. ▼

▲ I am a ward **clerk**. I make sure patient's **records** are kept up to date.

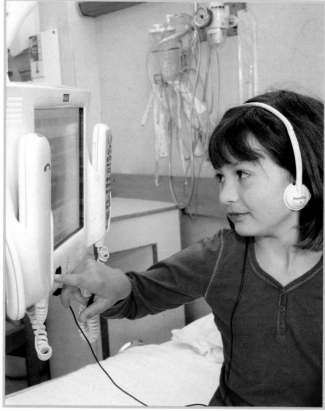

▲ Susannah is listening to the hospital radio.

◀ I am the hospital radio DJ. Patients can request songs to be played.

X-rays

Radiographers take x-ray pictures of patients when they come in for an operation. Patients need to lie very still so that a clear x-ray is taken.

I tell Mark that the x-ray will not hurt him. He will not feel a thing. ▶

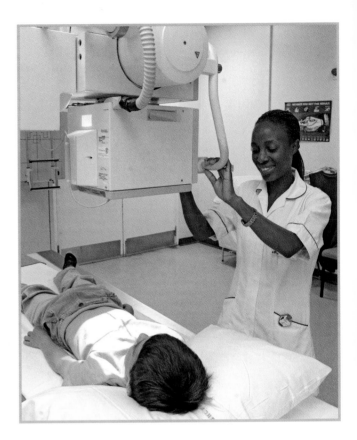

Then I position the camera over Mark's chest and make some final adjustments. ▼

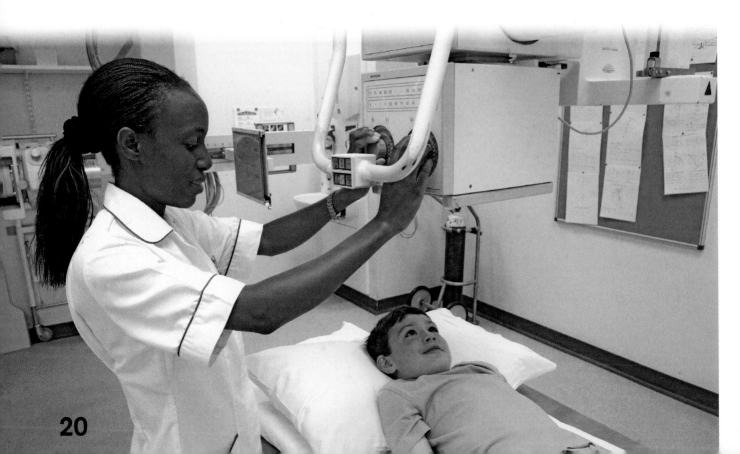

X-rays show the inside of a patient's body and help the doctors to find out what may be wrong.

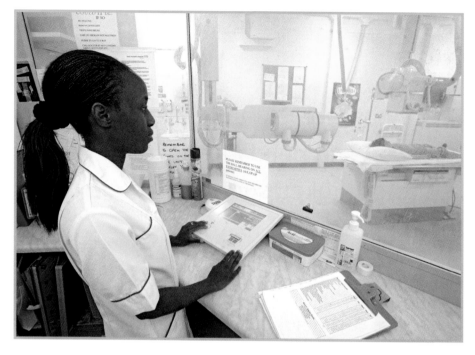

▲ I take the x-ray from inside another room.

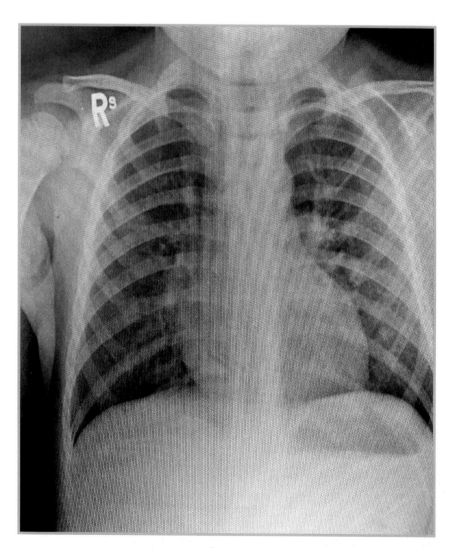

◀ The x-ray of Mark's chest instantly appears on a computer screen.

Before an operation

Susannah has come to the children's ward because she needs to have an operation. A doctor makes sure that she is ready to have the operation.

I am the doctor in charge of Susannah's treatment. I talk about how we will prepare Susannah for her operation. ▶

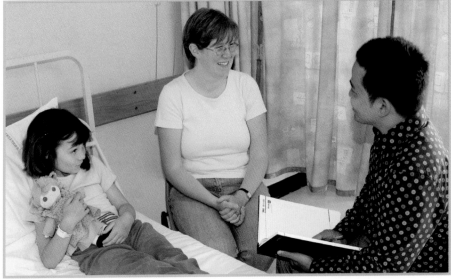

Patients cannot have anything to eat or drink before an operation. ▶

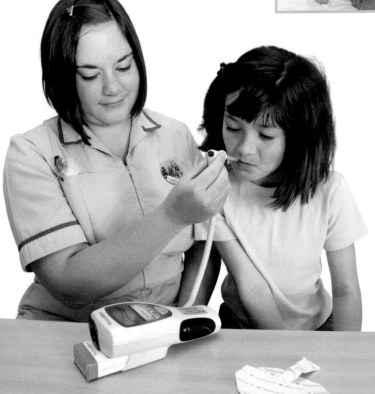

◀ Before the operation, I take Susannah's temperature.

There is all sorts of equipment used at the hospital.

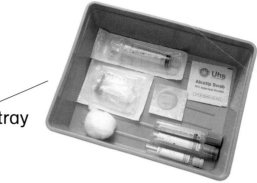

equipment tray

This is a cannula. It is put into a patient's vein, so doctors can give the patient the correct medicine.

digital thermometer

A stethoscope is used to check a patient's heartbeat and breathing.

A nurses watch is used to time a patient's **pulse**.

A mask is worn in the operating theatre to stop the spread of **germs**.

Latex gloves are always worn so that germs are not spread.

anaesthetic cream and clear sticky plasters

23

The operating theatre

An operating theatre is where patients go to have an operation. The doctors who do the operations are called surgeons.

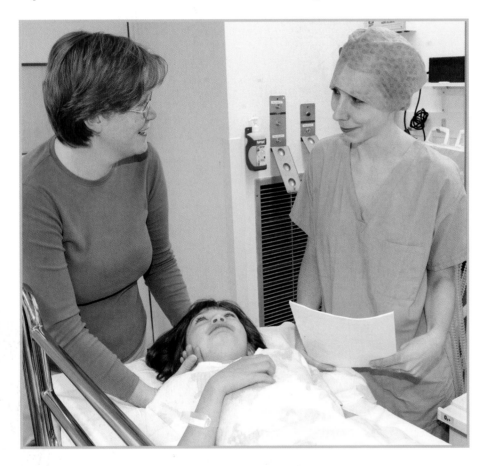

◀ I am a theatre nurse. I will get Susannah ready for her operation.

I attach a finger probe to Susannah's finger to monitor her throughout the operation. ▶

A doctor gives Susannah an anaesthetic to make her sleep throughout the operation.

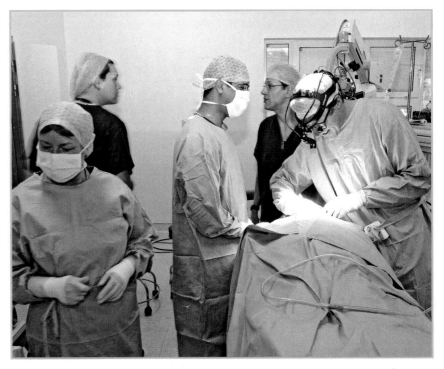

▲ All operating staff wear masks to help prevent the spread of germs.

Susannah's operation is over. I wake her up and make sure she is comfortable. ▼

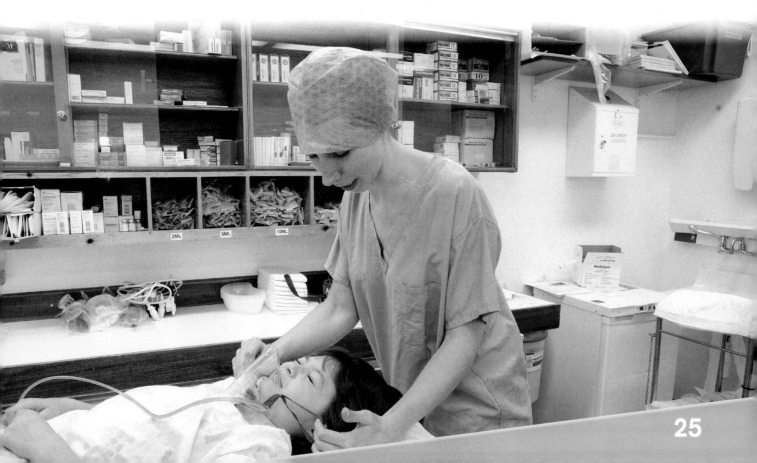

Going home

Patients leave the hospital when their doctor says they are well enough to go home.

I carefully remove the cannula from Susannah's hand. ▶

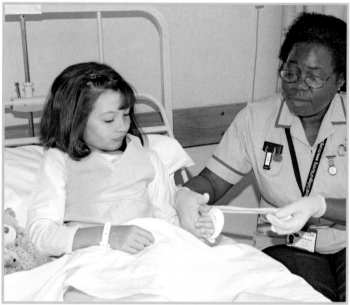

I give Susannah's mum a **prescription** for medicine to help her get better after her operation. ▼

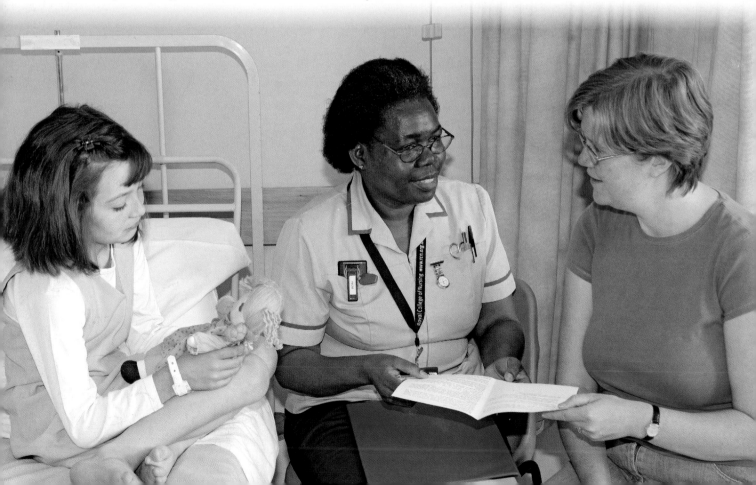

Susannah may need to come back to see her doctor in the **outpatients** department, to check that everything is going well.

Susannah and her mum pack her bags ready to go home. ▼

Glossary

anaesthetic a substance that puts a patient to sleep

ancillary staff support staff who help the doctors and nurses

cannula a tiny plastic tube that a patient wears in their hand

clerk a member of staff who keeps patient's records up to date

doctor someone who is qualified to practice medicine

germs tiny organisms which can cause illness or disease

hospital play specialists staff who reassure children and make their stay in the ward happy

numb when a patient cannot feel something

nurses staff that look after patients and help doctors

outpatients patients who come in for an appointment or operation and leave on the same day

prescription medicine that a doctor gives a patient

pulse a person's heartbeat, as felt through their wrist

radiographer staff who take x-rays of patients

records a patient's written details

register to sign in a patient

sample a small amount of something (like blood) that will later be tested

shifts doctors and nurses work day shifts and night shifts so that the patients are never left without care

stethoscope an instrument doctors use to listen to a patient's breathing and heartbeat

veins we all have veins inside our bodies that carry blood to our hearts

x-ray a picture that shows the inside of a patient's body

Quiz

Look back through the book to do this quiz.

1 What must every patient wear
  when they stay in hospital?

2 What are you not allowed to do
  before an operation?

3 What do nurses use to take a
  patient's temperature?

4 What is a cannula?

5 What is a hospital play
  specialist's job?

6 Who takes x-rays?

7 Why do staff in the operating
  theatre wear masks?

Answers

1 An identity wristband.
2 Eat or drink.
3 A thermometer.
4 A tiny plastic tube which is inserted
  into a vein in your hand.
5 To reassure children and make
  their stay in the ward as happy
  as possible.
6 A radiographer.
7 To help prevent the spread
  of germs.

Useful contacts

**www.kidshealth.org/kid/feel_
better/places/hospital.html**
Explains what goes on inside a hospital and
other health-related issues.

www.gosh.nhs.uk/
Joint website of Great Ormond Street Hospital
for Children NHS Trust and UCL Institute of
Child Health.

www.chelseachildrenshospitalschool.org/
A special school that provides classroom and
ward-based education on five hospital sites for
children while they are in hospital.

**We're here to
look after you!**

Index

ambulance 15

breathing 14, 23
blood 17, 24

children's ward 10-11,
  17, 18, 22

date of birth 9
doctor 6, 14-15,
  16, 21, 22, 23, 24,
  25, 26, 27

equipment 23

food 18

germs 23, 25

ill 6
injured 6

medicine 13, 23, 26

nameband 9
nurse 6, 8, 16-17, 23,
  24

operation 9, 12, 14,
  20, 22-23, 24-25, 26

parent 10
patient 8, 11, 14,
  15, 16, 18, 19, 20,
  22, 23, 24
progress 9, 14
pulse 23

radio 19
reception 8–9
records 19
register 8
relatives 16

shifts 15
stethoscope 14, 23
syringe 15

thermometer 23
treatment 16, 22

x-ray 15, 20-21

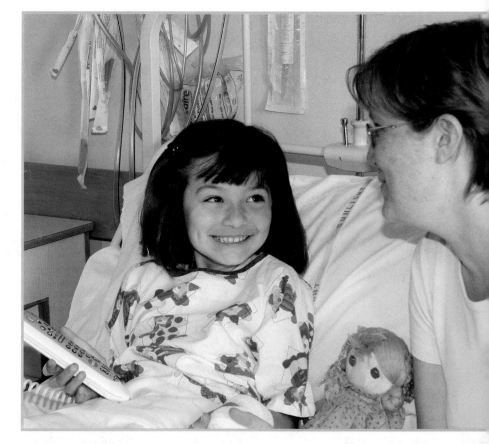